Nacho's
NACHOS

The Story Behind the World's Favorite Snack

by **SANDRA NICKEL**

illustrations by **OLIVER DOMINGUEZ**

Lee & Low Books Inc.   New York

LEE & LOW BOOKS INC.
95 Madison Avenue, New York, NY 10016
leeandlow.com

Edited by Louise E. May
Designed by Christy Hale
Produced by The Kids at Our House
The text is set in Zapf Renaissance
The illustrations are rendered in acrylic,
gouache, ink, and colored pencil
Manufactured in China at RR Donnelley
10 9 8 7 6 5 4 3 2 1
First Edition

Library of Congress Cataloging-in-Publication Data
Names: Nickel, Sandra, author. | Dominguez, Oliver, illustrator.
Title: Nacho's nachos : the story behind the world's favorite
snack / by Sandra Nickel ; illustrations by Oliver Dominguez.
Description: New York : Lee & Low Books, 2020. | Includes bibliographical
references. | Summary: "A picture book biography of Ignacio (Nacho) Anaya,
a waiter at the Victory Club in Piedras Negras, Coahuila, Mexico, and the
events surrounding the creation, in 1940, of the globally-popular tortilla chip,
cheese, and jalapeño pepper snack that bears his name: nachos"
— Provided by publisher.
Identifiers: LCCN 2019031147 | ISBN 9781620143698 (hardcover)
Subjects: LCSH: Anaya, Ignacio, 1895-1975. | Nachos—Juvenile literature. |
Waiters—Mexico—Biography—Juvenile literature. | Restaurateurs—Texas—
Biography—Juvenile literature.
Classification: LCC TX740 .N53 2020 | DDC 641.81/2—dc23
LC record available at https://lccn.loc.gov/2019031147

To the families of Ignacio Anaya, Mamie Finan,
and Rodolfo de los Santos —*S.N.*

To my kids, Aubrey and Gage! —*O.D.*

In 1895, a baby boy was born in northern Mexico. His name was Ignacio Anaya, and like a lot of Ignacios, he was called Nacho for short.

Nacho's parents died when he was young, and he went to live with a foster mother. He loved to sit in the kitchen while she made quesadillas. She warmed corn tortillas, folded cheese inside, and toasted them until they were golden on the outside and melted on the inside. Nacho ate up one quesadilla after the other.

Nacho learned about cooking from his foster mother. As he grew older, he became quite good at other tasks around the kitchen too.

When Nacho turned twenty-three, he found a job at a restaurant. He was willing to do whatever was needed: seat guests, pass out menus, take orders, and serve meals. As Nacho went from table to table, people smiled. He had a special talent for making diners happy.

In the Mexican city of Piedras Negras, Rodolfo de los Santos heard about Nacho. Rodolfo was opening a new restaurant, the Victory Club, right across the Rio Grande river from Eagle Pass, Texas, in the United States.

The Club Victoria, as the restaurant was called in Spanish, had its own orchestra, a Moonlight Patio for dancing, and four different menus featuring everything from steaks to seafood to Mexican specialties. Rodolfo wanted the best music, the best food, and the best people—and that included Nacho.

The Victory Club's customers came from both Mexico and the United States. When they arrived, Nacho made sure everyone felt welcome. Nacho even knew how to please Mamie Finan.

Mamie lived in Eagle Pass, but she was known on both sides of the border for her outstanding cooking. At home she served guests jalapeño jelly, French crepes, and oyster soup. At the Victory Club, she wanted to try new dishes.

One afternoon in 1940 during the Victory Club's quiet hours between lunch and dinner, Mamie walked in with three friends.

"Nacho, we're tired of the usual type snacks," Mamie said. "Do you think you could whip us up something new? Something different?"

Nacho smiled and headed for the kitchen.

But Nacho had a problem. He didn't have any idea what to make. Even worse, there wasn't a single cook in the kitchen, and Rodolfo was nowhere to be seen.

Nacho threw open the doors of the cupboards. He searched in the refrigerator. Finally he spotted some freshly fried pieces of corn tortillas in a bowl and got an idea.

Nacho carefully spread out
the tortilla pieces on a platter.

He sprinkled them
with Cheddar cheese,

and topped each piece
of tortilla with a strip of
pickled jalapeño pepper.

As a last touch, he put the
tortillas in the oven until they
were golden and melted, just like
his foster mother's quesadillas.

Nacho rushed the hot platter out of the kitchen and placed it on the table. Mamie picked up a tortilla and took a bite.

Hot, crispy tortilla. Melted Cheddar cheese. A slice of jalapeño.

So simple! So scrumptious! So spectacular!

"What do you call these snacks?" asked Mamie.

Nacho grinned. "Well, I guess we can just call them Nacho's Special," he said.

Mamie and her friends ordered another platter . . . and another. They ate until not a single bit of the crispy new snack was left.

When the women finally left a couple of hours later, Nacho had already gone home. But on their way out of the Victory Club, the women came across friend after friend arriving for dinner. They told everyone to order the delicious new dish, Nacho's Special.

As soon as Nacho arrived at work the next day, waiters crowded around him. They wanted to know what Nacho's Special was. Customers had been asking for it since the night before.

Nacho headed straight into the kitchen and started cooking.

Rodolfo watched his customers eat.
Nacho made people smile when he served
them as a waiter. But their smiles were even bigger
when they ate Nacho's cooking.

Rodolfo promoted Nacho to executive chef and put
him in charge of making diners happy. He also added
Nacho's new dish to every Victory Club menu.

Year after year, word of Nacho's Special spread. Restaurants all over Mexico and the United States began to serve the dish. Some added beans, some added guacamole, and somewhere along the way, restaurants started calling the dish simply "nachos."

People still traveled to Piedras Negras. They wanted to eat nachos in the city where they were invented. Even a president of the United States and famous Mexican and American actors came to try the crunchy, cheesy, spicy snack!

When the Victory Club closed in 1961, Nacho decided to open a restaurant of his own. He found a place in Piedras Negras, set up tables and chairs, wrote out his menu, and made sure to have plenty of tortillas, Cheddar cheese, and jalapeño peppers on hand.

Once everything was ready, he put up his sign in front of the door.

He called his restaurant Nacho's, and his most popular dish was, of course, Nacho's nachos!

ORIGINAL NACHOS

Children will need adult help with this recipe.

5 fresh corn tortillas cut into quarters and fried,
   or 20 large corn tortilla chips
2 cups grated Cheddar cheese
20 pickled jalapeño pepper strips*

measuring cup
large baking sheet
measuring spoons
potholders or oven mitts

1. Preheat the oven to 450°F.

2. Spread out the chips in a single layer on the baking sheet.

3. Top each chip with a rounded tablespoon of cheese and one jalapeño strip.

4. Bake the prepared nachos in the preheated oven for 4 minutes or until the cheese is melted.

5. Use potholders or oven mitts to remove the nachos from the oven.

6. Let the nachos cool for 2 minutes. Then dig in and enjoy!

Makes five servings of four pieces each.

*Jalapeños are spicy chili peppers. If you cannot find pickled strips of jalapeños, use pickled rounds. And if spicy is not for you, try something milder, such as pickled banana peppers.

AFTERWORD

Ignacio Anaya García was born in San Carlos, Chihuahua, Mexico, in 1895. He worked in restaurants in San Angelo, Texas, in the United States and in Ciudad Acuña, Chihuahua, before moving to Piedras Negras, Coahuila. Nacho served his first platter of Nacho's Special at the Victory Club in 1940. Many people came to Piedras Negras and tried the original nachos at Rodolfo's or Nacho's restaurant, including US President Lyndon B. Johnson, American actor John Wayne, and Mexican actors Cantinflas and Ricardo Montalbán. Nacho's famous invention was so popular, it spread

Ignacio (Nacho) Anaya with his daughter Norma and his grandchildren Luis (top), Evangeline (left), and Rosa Martha, ca. 1963

Photo courtesy of Norma Anaya

around the world. Today people can order nachos at all types of restaurants, sports stadiums, movie theaters, and snack bars everywhere from New York to Tokyo and beyond. Sometimes beans, guacamole, sour cream, beef, and/or chicken are added. But the original Nacho's Special, as invented by Nacho, consists only of fried tortilla pieces with melted Cheddar cheese and strips of pickled jalapeños on top. Jalapeños were originally pickled whole or in strips and only later in rounds, as they are commonly seen today.

Mamie Finan was born in 1887 in Hillsboro, Texas. When she was sixteen, she moved to Mexico with her parents. She was married there, ranched with her husband, and survived outlaws surrounding their home. After her husband died, she moved to Eagle Pass, Texas, right across the border from the Victory Club, and began selling insurance.

Rodolfo de los Santos opened his first restaurant, El Moderno, when he was twenty-two years old. He used the money he earned to help support his mother, brothers, and sisters. Around 1939, he opened the Victory Club in Piedras Negras, where Nacho eventually worked for more than twenty years. Rodolfo was so grateful to Nacho for his many years of service, he gave Nacho kitchen equipment for his own new restaurant when the Victory Club closed.

Over time, the word *Special* was dropped from the name of the snack, as was the apostrophe in *Nacho's*. Most people around the world don't know that there was a real person—a man named Nacho—who created the popular dish. The city of Piedras Negras, however, never forgot. Every year around October 21, when International Day of the Nacho is celebrated, Piedras Negras throws a three-day Nacho Fest with music, games, and best of all, lots and lots of nachos.

AUTHOR'S NOTE and ACKNOWLEDGMENTS

As often happens with stories told by word of mouth, many versions of Nacho's story exist. Some say Nacho invented his famous snack at El Moderno or Ma Crosby's in Ciudad Acuña. Some say Mamie brought ten to twelve military wives with her to the Victory Club. One version even says Nacho served the first nachos to a group of soldiers! The story I have told here is based on the earliest telling I could find, a newspaper article from 1954, for which the reporter interviewed Nacho himself. I filled in the details from a later article, and from information I gathered during a visit to Piedras Negras and Eagle Pass, and through communications with descendants of Ignacio Anaya, Mamie Finan, and Rodolfo de los Santos. I am very grateful to Luis Ignacio Anaya, Marcela Anaya, Norma Anaya, Alana Avery, Evita Avery, Patricia Finan de los Santos, Rodolfo de los Santos Jr., Sandra Martinez of the Eagle Pass Chamber of Commerce, and the Oficina de Convenciones y Visitantes de Piedras Negras for their generosity in helping me get as close as possible to the way things really happened.

QUOTATION SOURCES

page 12: "Nacho, we're . . . Something different?" Ignacio Anaya, quoted in Clarence J. LaRoche, "Nacho's? Natch!" *San Antonio Express and San Antonio News* (May 23, 1954): 3H.

page 19: "What do . . . snacks?" Ibid.
"Well, I . . . Nacho's Special." Ibid.

back cover: "I didn't . . . Saudi Arabia." Ignacio Anaya, quoted in Bill Salter, "'Nacho' Inventor Hasn't Profited." *San Antonio Express and News* (June 15, 1969): 97.

AUTHOR'S SOURCES

Anaya, Luis Ignacio (grandson of Ignacio Anaya), e-mail correspondence with the author, October 2016–November 2019.

Anaya, Marcela (granddaughter of Ignacio Anaya), text message to the author, September 28, 2016.

Avery, Alana (great-granddaughter of Mamie Finan), personal interview with the author, November 10, 2016.

Avery, Evita (granddaughter of Mamie Finan), email correspondence with the author, September 1, 2016.

de los Santos, Patricia Finan (granddaughter of Mamie Finan), personal interview with the author, October 2, 2016; email correspondence with the author, October 2016–November 2019.

de los Santos Jr., Rodolfo (son of Rodolfo de los Santos), personal interview with the author, October 2, 2016; email correspondence with the author, October 2016–September 2019.

Finan, Mamie T. Interview by Sarah E. John, November 11, 1977, interview 341. Institute of Oral History, University of Texas at El Paso. https://digitalcommons.utep.edu/interviews/341/.

LaRoche, Clarence J. "Nacho's? Natch!" *San Antonio Express and San Antonio News*, May 23, 1954: 3H. Accessed by subscription. https://newspaperarchive.com.

Peña de los Santos, Adalberto, and Romina Mendoza (representatives of the Oficina de Convenciones y Visitantes de Piedras Negras, Coahuila, Mexico), personal interview with the author, October 1, 2016.

Rodríguez, Josué. "Arranca en Piedras Negras el internacional 'Nacho Fest'; esperan 25 mil personas." Vanguardia, MX, October 12, 2016. https://vanguardia.com.mx/articulo/arranca-en-piedras-negras-el-internacional-nacho-fest-0.

Salter, Bill. "'Nacho' Inventor Hasn't Profited." *San Antonio Express and News*, June 15, 1969: 97. Accessed by subscription. https://newspaperarchive.com.

Victory Club Advertisement. *Crystal City Zavala County Sentinel*, May 11, 1956. Accessed by subscription. https://newspaperarchive.com.